THE
SPOOKTACULAR
JOKE BOOK

POLLY T GEIST

Illustrated by
Alan Rowe

Knight Books
HODDER & STOUGHTON

Text copyright © Complete Editions
1992
Illustrations copyright © Alan Rowe
1992

First published in Great Britain in
1992

*The characters and situations in this
book are entirely imaginary and bear
no relation to any real person or
actual happenings.*

The rights of Polly T. Geist to be
identified as the author of the text of
this work and of Alan Rowe to be
identified as the illustrator of this
work, has been asserted by them in
accordance with the Copyright,
Designs and Patents Act 1988.

This book is sold subject to the condition that it shall not, by way of trade
or otherwise, be lent, re-sold, hired
out or otherwise circulated without
the publisher's prior consent in any
form of binding or cover other than
that in which it is published and
without a similar condition including
this condition being imposed on the
subsequent purchaser.

No part of this publication may be
reproduced or transmitted in any
form or by any means, electronic or
mechanical, including photo-
copying, recording or any
information storage or retrieval
system, without either the prior
permission in writing from the
publisher or a licence, permitting
restricted copying. In the United
Kingdom such licences are issued by
the Copyright Licensing Agency, 90
Tottenham Court Road, London W1P
9HE.

Printed and bound in Great Britain
for Hodder and Stoughton Paper-
backs, a division of Hodder and
Stoughton Ltd, Mill Road, Dunton
Green, Sevenoaks, Kent TN13 2YA.
(Editorial Office: 47 Bedford Square,
London WC1B 3DP) by Clays Ltd,
St Ives plc. Photoset by Rowland
Phototypesetting Ltd, Bury St
Edmunds, Suffolk.

British Library C.I.P.
A catalogue record for this book is
available from the British Library

ISBN 0-340-56579-9

Contents

It's a scream!

INTRODUCTION

Are you b-b-brave enough to read *The Sp-Sp Spooktacular Joke Book?* It's a spine-chilling, teeth-chattering, funny-bone-tickling collection of ghostly giggles, packed with ghosts, ghouls, spooks, phantoms, vampires, skeletons, monsters, witches, zombies and lots of other nasty creatures. Frightful, fearsom and extremely funny, they'll make you shake in your shoes – with laughter, of course!

Polly.T.Geist

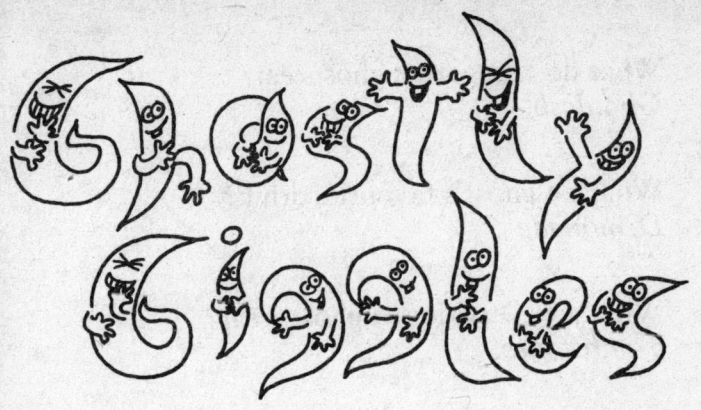

Ghostly Giggles

What would you do if a ghost came through
your front door?
Run out of the back door!

What game do ghosts play at parties?
Haunt and seek.

Which ghost has the best hearing?
The eeriest.

PETER: I met a ghost last night.
ZITA: What did it say?
PETER: I don't know, I can't speak dead
languages.

MOTHER GHOST TO CHILD: Be quiet, and
only spook when you're spoken to.

How does a ghost-hunter keep fit?
Regular exorcise.

What do Hungarian ghosts eat?
Ghoulash.

What's a ghost's favourite drink?
Demonade.

What jewellery does a ghost wear?
Tombstones.

FIRST GHOST: You look tired.
SECOND GHOST: Yes, I'm dead on my feet.

Why do spooks like riding horses?
They like ghoulloping.

Who writes a spook's biography?
A *ghost writer*.

Where do ghosts catch the train?
Manifestation.

What did the Egyptian mummy say when she
sent her son off to school?
'*Wrap up well, dear*.'

Did you hear about the ghost who took off from
Gatwick?
He was on a night fright.

Where do ghosts live?
In a far-off terror-tory.

FIRST GHOST: You give me eerie ache!
SECOND GHOST: Sorry I spook.

How do ghosts count?
*One, boo, three, four, five, six, seven, hate, nine,
frighten*.

What do young ghosts like chewing?
Booble gum.

GHOSTLY MOTTO: Home is where you hang
your head.

JENNY: I keep thinking I'm a ghost.
BENNY: I wondered why you walked in through the wall.

What do you get if you cross an Egyptian mummy with a motor mechanic?
A toot and car man.

What screams more loudly than a girl frightened by a ghost?
Two girls frightened by ghosts.

What's a ghost's final drink?
His bier.

An ancient old ghost of Devizes
Had ears of different sizes.
The one that was small
Was no use at all,
But the other won several prizes.

What happened to the Arab when he saw a ghost?
He became the Shake of Arabia.

What's a ghost after it's 150 years old?
151 years old.

If you throw eggs at a ghost, do you eggsterminate him?

What happened when the cow saw a ghost?
She gave milk shakes.

What's the name of the overweight ghost who haunts London's Covent Garden?
The Fat-Tum of the Opera.

FIRST GHOST: I had trouble breathing.
SECOND GHOST: What happened?
FIRST GHOST: The doctor gave me something to stop it.

Why was the Egyptian child worried?
Because his daddy was a mummy.

Is a mummy good at keeping secrets?
Yes, it likes to keep things under wraps.

What happens when a mummy eats biscuits in bed?
You get a crumby mummy.

What do you find in a haunted cellar?
Whines and spirits.

FIRST GHOST: I've played the piano for 100 years, on and off.
SECOND GHOST: Slippery stool?

FIRST GHOST: I've been told I have music in my feet.
SECOND GHOST: Yes, two flats.

What kind of girl does a mummy go out with?
Any old girl he can dig up.

What happens if a ghost eats the Christmas decorations?
He gets tinselitis.

How do spooks get to work?
On ghost trains.

What's it called when ghosts star in a TV show?
A spooktacular.

Where was the ghost when the lights went out?
In the dark.

Why did the ghost pianist have a piano in his bathroom?
He liked to play Handel's 'Water Music'.

GERALD: You can tell that ghost was a careful driver.
GLORIA: How?
GERALD: He's got wing mirrors.

Did you hear that the annual conference of clairvoyants has been cancelled due to unforeseen circumstances?

FIRST GHOST: When I died I left my brain for science.
SECOND GHOST: I suppose every little helps.

There once was a phantom called Pete
Who never could play, drink or eat.
Said he, 'I don't care
For a bun or éclair,
Can't you see that I'm dead on my feet?'

What wears a sheet and lights up?
An electric ghost.

Knock, knock.
Who's there?
Hugo.
Hugo who?
Hugo first, I'm scared!

Why did the mummy leave his tomb after 5000 years?
He thought he was old enough to leave home.

What kind of fish does a ghost fish for?
Angel fish.

Who plays in goal when ghosts play football?
The ghoullie, of course.

What do ghosts who've been in hospital like
doing?
Talking about their apparitions.

How do you make a ghost shiver?
Tell it a people story.

Where do ghosts send their laundry?
To the dry screamers.

How does a Hawaiian ghost laugh?
A low ha.

FIRST GHOST: Arrivederci.
SECOND GHOST: What's that?
FIRST GHOST: 'Goodbye' in Italian.
SECOND GHOST: Strychnine.
FIRST GHOST: What's that?
SECOND GHOST: 'Goodbye' in any language.

ZOMBIE TO VISITOR: Don't sit in that chair, it's for rigor mortis to set in.

How can you tell a musical ghost?
He fiddles with his beard.

Knock, knock.
Who's there?
Dishes.
Dishes who?
Dishes a ghost, open up!

What do mummies wear on their fingernails?
Nile varnish.

Which ghost was friendly with the three bears?
Ghouldilocks.

Lady Jane Grey
Had little to say.
What could she have said
After losing her head?

When do ghosts haunt skyscrapers?
When they're in high spirits.

GIRL GHOST: Do you believe in the hereafter?
BOY GHOST: Yes.
GIRL GHOST: Well, hereafter leave me alone!

FIRST GHOST: What's the difference between
a sheet and a person?
SECOND GHOST: One I wear, the other I was.

Where do spooks study?
Ghoullege.

What do you call ghost children?
Boys and ghouls.

How does a ghost begin a letter?
'Tomb it may concern.'

Did you hear about the stupid ghost who climbed *over* walls?

What do ghosts have on roast beef?
Grave-y.

GHOST OF HENRY VIII: I'm glad I'm not alive today.
GHOST OF ANNE BOLEYN: Why?
GHOST OF HENRY VIII: There'd be a lot more history to learn!

Where do ghosts swim?
In the Dead Sea.

What did the phantom guard say?
'Who ghosts there?'

What do you get if you cross a tin of food with
a spook?
Beans on ghost.

HARRY: What would you do if your bedroom
was haunted?
BARRY: Sleep somewhere else!

What do Italian ghosts eat?
Spook-hetti.

Knock, knock.
Who's there?
Zombies.
Zombies who?
Zombies make honey.

FIRST GHOST: I had a milk bath last night.
SECOND GHOST: Pasteurised?
FIRST GHOST: No, just up to my waist.

Why is seeing a ghost like hot water?
Because it's not so hot once you get used to it.

Two children were looking at a mummy in a museum. '2000 BC, says the sign,' said one, 'what does that mean?'

'It's probably the number plate of the car that ran him over,' replied the second.

Knock, knock.
Who's there?
Boo.
Boo who?
Boo I'm a ghost, but don't cry!

What's a ghost's favourite order?
A postal order.

What was the ghost who painted himself with gold paint suffering from?
A gilt complex.

If a ghost faints, what number does he need?
Someone to bring him 2.

What did the ghost do when he got his gas bill?
Exploded!

A funny old phantom called Rose
Had a very big wart on her nose.
When she had it removed
Her appearance improved,
But her glasses slipped down to her toes.

FIRST GHOST: Will I lose my looks as I get more invisible?
SECOND GHOST: I hope so!

What did the ghost policeman say to his stomach?
I've got you under a vest.

Why do nervous ghosts not play the harp?
It takes a lot of pluck.

What do ghosts like for breakfast?
Dreaded Wheat.

Did you hear about the ghost intruder?
He got intruder window.

Who said, 'Shiver me timbers!' on the ghost ship?
The skeleton crew.

ZOMBIE: Am I all right for the zoo?
BUS CONDUCTOR: With your face, certainly.

FIRST GHOST: Boo-ooo-ooo-ooo.
SECOND GHOST: Bark, bark.
FIRST GHOST: What do you mean, 'Bark, bark'?
FIRST GHOST: I'm learning a foreign language.

MARTHA: I hear you saw a spiritualist. Was he any good?
MERVYN: Oh, medium.

22

ANNE: Did you hear about the man who didn't know the meaning of the word 'fear'?
DAN: How was that?
ANNE: He was too afraid to ask.

FIRST GHOST: What are you doing?
SECOND GHOST: Writing a letter to myself.
FIRST GHOST: What does it say?
SECOND GHOST: I won't know until I get it tomorrow.

What did the ghost with poor eyesight wear?
Spooktacles.

GRAVE HUMOUR

How can you avoid dying?
It's quite simple — you stay in the living-room.

What's another name for a funeral parlour?
A departure lounge.

HARRY: I hear you buried your Grandad last week.
LARRY: Had to. He was dead, you know.

What did one casket say to the other?
'Is that you coffin?'

Where does an undertaker work?
In a box office.

MRS ADDLE: Does your husband have life insurance?
MRS BADDLE: No, fire insurance. He says he knows where he's going.

How do undertakers work out the cost of a funeral?
By dead reckoning.

FIRST GARDENER: I used to work with hundreds of people under me.
SECOND GARDENER: Where?
FIRST GARDENER: In the cemetery.

'If you like grave humour I might tell you the joke about the body snatchers. On second thoughts, I don't think I will. You might get carried away.'

How did the Egyptian worm catch a cold?
From its mummy.

INVITATION: The cremation of Mr Henry Higgins will take place at Greenwater Crematorium at noon.
REPLY: Put him on a low gas, I can't make it until 3 pm.

NURSE: How many operations has that new doctor done? Is it five?
COLLEAGUE: No, six. I've been to all the funerals.

What's an undertaker's motto?
The morgue the merrier.

'Doctor, doctor, I've only got 59 seconds to live. . . !'
'Just hang on a minute . . .'

Down the street his funeral goes,
As sobs and wails diminish.
He died from drinking varnish,
But he had a lovely finish.

ADVERTISEMENT: For sale, 1930s hearse. Original body.

Why can you never trust an undertaker?
Because eventually he'll let you down.

KEN: Did you hear they're putting a fence round the cemetery?
BEN: No. Why's that?
KEN: People were dying to get in.

MAN ON PHONE: A box for four, please.
MAN ANSWERING PHONE: I'm sorry, we only have boxes for one.
MAN ON PHONE: Is that the Adelphi Theatre?
MAN ANSWERING PHONE: No, it's Smith's the Undertakers.

What happened to the undertaker who died?
He went and buried himself in the country.

What do you have to do to become a coroner?
Pass stiff exams.

How does an undertaker look when he's worried?
Very grave.

NEWS ITEM: Mrs Shufflebottom discovered her husband dead in the garden and curried his body indoors.

CLIENT: Please bury my wife.
UNDERTAKER: But I buried your wife last year.
CLIENT: I remarried.
UNDERTAKER: Congratulations, sir.

'Doctor, doctor, I feel half dead.'
'We'll arrange for you to be buried up to the waist.'

'Doctor, doctor, I feel I'm at death's door.'
'Don't worry, I'll soon pull you through.'

HETTIE: Have you heard about the new DIY funerals?
LETTIE: No, what are they?
HETTIE: They loosen the earth and you sink down by yourself.

FIRST DRIVER: I get tired of people complaining from the back seat.
SECOND DRIVER: I've been driving for years and never once had a word of complaint from the back seat.
FIRST DRIVER: What do you drive then? Not a taxi?
SECOND DRIVER: No, a hearse.

SALLY: My grandad has one foot in the grate.
WALLY: Don't you mean the grave?
SALLY: No, the grate. He wants to be cremated.

Why should you go to a graveyard if you're lonely?
Because there's always some body there.

What did one corpse say to another?
'Em-balmy about you.'

The man who makes me does not need me. The
man who buys me does not use me himself. The
man who uses me does so without knowing.
What am I?
A coffin.

Why are graveyards noisy places?
Because of all the coffin.

How does an undertaker fasten his tie?
With a wreath knot.

What's the underneath of a graveyard called?
A spirit level.

What's an undertaker's favourite town?
Gravesend.

How can you tell an undertaker?
By his grave manner.

What's an undertaker's favourite saying?
'Every shroud has a silver lining.'

What's an undertaker's least favourite saying?
'Never say die.'

Where do undertakers go on outings?
The Hearse of the Year Show.

What killed the undertaker?
His coffin.

Epitaphs

Beneath this stone, a lump of clay,
Lies Major Peter Daniels.
Who, early in the month of May
Took off his winter flannels.

Little Willie,
Pair of skates,
Hole in ice —
Pearly gates.

The manner of her death was thus —
She was run over by a bus.

Here lies our M.P. —
He's lying still.

Grim death took me without any warning.
I was well at night and dead in the morning.

It wasn't the cough that carried him off —
It was the coffin they carried him off in.

Here lies the body of Mick O'Shea
Who died maintaining his right of way.
His case was clear and his will was strong,
But he's as dead as if he'd been wrong.

ON A DENTIST'S TOMB: Stranger, approach
this spot with gravity — Bill Smith's filling his
last cavity.

Here lies a chap who got no gain
By jumping from a moving train.
Banana skins on Platform 7
Ensured his terminus was heaven.

RATTLING GOOD TIME

Why do skeletons like milk?
It's good for the bones.

What's a skeleton's favourite pop group?
Bony M.

Who looks after a haunted house?
A skeleton staff.

What goes 'Ha, ha, ha, thump!'
A skeleton laughing its head off.

What did the skeleton do when it lost a hand?
Went to a second-hand shop.

What do skeletons sell at garden parties?
Rattle tickets.

What was the skeleton's favourite pop song?
'Shake, Rattle and Roll.'

What do you do if you see a skeleton out
jogging?
Jump out of your skin and join him.

Why didn't the skeleton enjoy the party?
Because everyone hung their coats on him.

What do you get if you cross a skeleton with a cobra?
A rattlesnake.

What did the skeleton say when the ghost asked to borrow £5 from him?
'Sorry, I'm skint.'

What's the definition of noise?
A skeleton tap dancing on a tin roof.

What *is* a skeleton?
Someone inside with his outside off.

Why can't skeletons fight?
They haven't any guts.

What do you call a skeleton who goes out in winter without wearing a hat?
A numbskull.

What do you call a friendly skeleton?
A bony crony.

Why was the skeleton no good at his job?
His heart wasn't in it.

How did the skeleton know there would be a thunderstorm?
He could feel it in his bones.

What do you call a detective skeleton?
Sherlock Bones.

When do skeletons' teeth chatter?
When they're chilled to the marrow.

What's a Scottish skeleton called?
Bony Prince Charlie.

What's a French skeleton called?
Napoleon Bone-apart.

What happened when the skeleton fell off a chair?
He got rattled.

What's a skeleton's favourite vegetable?
Marrow.

How do you make a skeleton laugh?
Tickle his funny bone.

Why didn't the skeleton enjoy the dance?
He had no body to dance with.

What instrument does a skeleton play?
The trom-bone.

What did the ghost call the skeleton?
Bonehead.

What do you call a skeleton who sits around all day doing nothing?
Lazy bones.

What is Dracula's favourite dance?
The Last Vaults.

What could the vampire waiter never serve?
Steak (stake).

'Mummy, Mummy, what's a vampire?'
'Shut up and drink your soup before it clots.'

Did you hear about the vampire's bike that went round and round biting people?
It was called a vicious cycle.

What's a young male vampire called?
Bat Boy.

Why does Dracula live in a coffin?
The rent's low.

What do you get if you cross a werewolf with a Christmas card?
Best vicious of the season.

'Mummy, Mummy, Daddy says I'm a werewolf!'
'Be quiet and go and comb your face.'

Did you hear about the werewolf that fell in a washing-machine?
It became a wash 'n' werewolf.

What is Dracula's favourite film?
The Vampire Strikes Back.

FIRST VAMPIRE: A tramp stopped me and said he hadn't had a bite for days.
SECOND VAMPIRE: What did you do?
FIRST VAMPIRE: I bit him.

NEWS ITEM: 'There is no question of my marrying Veronica Vampire,' says Count Dracula. 'We are just good fiends.'

Why did Dracula carry his coffin around with him?
Because his life was at stake.

Did you hear about the stupid werewolf that lay down to chew a bone?
When it stood up it only had three legs.

Where does Dracula go in New York?
The Vampire State Building.

What did the vampire call a set of dentures?
A new-fangled device.

What's Dracula's favourite slogan?
Give blood generously.

What did the werewolf say to his victim?
'It's been nice gnawing you.'

GRAFFITI: Dracula loved in vein.
I'm a vampire, please wash your neck.

HOLLY: Can a vampire with no teeth bite you?
MOLLY: No, but he can give you a nasty suck.

If Dracula knocked out a boxer, what would he be?
Out for the Count.

What do you get if you cross a vampire with a telescope?
A horrorscope.

MOTHER WEREWOLF: Could you go upstairs, dear, the baby's howling again.

Have you read *Life Among the Werewolves* by Norah Bone?

Why did Dracula's wife leave him?
Because he was a pain in the neck.

ADVERTISEMENT: Join Dracula's Fan Club. Just send your name, address and blood sample.

What is Dracula's favourite song?
'Fangs for the Memory.'

Which song does Dracula hate?
'Peg O' My Heart.'

What did the vampire say when it saw a knight in armour?
'Oh, no, not tinned food again.'

What do vampires eat with bread and cheese?
Pickled organs.

LADY: Your little boy bit my ankle!
VAMPIRE: That's because he's not tall enough to bite your neck.

Why is it cheap to keep a vampire?
He eats necks to nothing.

Why did Dracula eat peppermints?
Because he had bat breath.

DON: What did you think of that Dracula film?
RON: Oh, fangtastic!

Where does a vampire keep his money?
In a blood bank.

What's a vampire's favourite soup?
Scream of tomato.

Why are vampire families close?
Because blood is thicker than water.

How does Dracula keep fit?
He plays batminton.

'Mummy, am I real vampire?'
'Yes, dear, why do you ask?'
'Because I faint every time I see blood.'

What do baby vampires say at bedtime?
'Read me a gory.'

What do vampires like for breakfast?
Ready Neck.

What's a vampire's favourite fruit?
Blood oranges.

FIRST VAMPIRE: Is Dracula a blood relative?
SECOND VAMPIRE: The bloodiest there is.

Why did Mrs Vampire never leave Mr Vampire?
She couldn't bear to kiss him goodbye.

Why is it easy to play a trick on a vampire?
They're all suckers.

What does a vampire do at 10.30 each morning?
Takes a coffin break.

What do vampire pop fans do?
Form a fang club.

What did the vampire say when the hairdresser cut his neck?
'Never mind, it's not my blood.'

What do you call a stupid vampire?
A silly clot.

How can you tell when a vampire is angry?
He flips his lid.

What do you call a short vampire?
A pain in the leg.

Why are vampires crazy?
Because they're bats.

What happened when the boy vampire met the girl vampire?
It was love at first bite.

What does a vampire say after he's bitten his victim?
'Fangs a lot.'

Why is Dracula keen on recruiting young vampires?
He likes to see new blood in the business.

What do vampires enjoy before going to bed?
A blood bath.

What do you call a vampire that has feathers and a beak, and swims on a boating lake?
Count Duckula.

Where does a vampire get his jokes from?
A crypt writer.

What kept Dracula's wife awake?
His coffin.

FIRST VAMPIRE: I've swallowed some blood the wrong way!
SECOND VAMPIRE: Are you choking?
FIRST VAMPIRE: No, I'm serious!

What was Dracula before he married Mrs Dracula?
A bat-chelor.

What happens to vampires in the rain?
They get wet.

Why do vampires go to Earls Court?
To see the Bat Show.

What's a vampire's favourite dance?
The fangdango.

How do vampires travel?
By blood vessel.

Why is it foolish to upset a cannibal?
You might find yourself in hot water.

Why should you keep calm if you meet a cannibal?
It's no good getting into a stew.

What happened when the two cannibal tribes were at war?
The winning side made mincemeat of the other.

What's a cannibal's favourite party game?
Swallow My Leader.

FIRST CANNIBAL: I don't know what to make of my husband.
SECOND CANNIBAL: How about a hotpot?

Have you read *The Cannibal's Daughter* by Henrietta Mann?

Let's face it, jokes about cannibals are in very poor taste!

How can you help a starving cannibal?
Give him a hand.

What's a cannibal's favourite dish?
Grilled chaps.

Is a cannibal who eats his father's sister an aunt-eater?

What's a definition of a cannibal?
A man who goes into a restaurant and orders the waiter.

'Mummy, Mummy, I hate Daddy's guts!'
'Shut up and eat what's on your plate.'

FIRST CANNIBAL: Who was that lady I saw you with last night?
SECOND CANNIBAL: That was no lady, that was my dinner.

What did the cannibal say when he met the famous explorer?
'Dr Livingstone, I consume.'

Did you hear about the cannibal who liked to stop where they serve coach parties?

Why was the cannibal secretary sacked?
Because she kept buttering up her boss.

What are a cannibal's favourite beans?
Human beans.

What did the cannibal say when he saw the sleeping missionary?
'Ah, breakfast in bed.'

Two cannibals went to a lecture. It was on 'How to serve your fellow man'.

A cannibal took a trip on a cruise liner. At dinner the first night the steward asked politely, 'Would you like to see the menu, sir?'

    'No, thanks,' replied the cannibal. 'Just bring me the passenger list.'

FIRST CANNIBAL: I don't like our maths teacher.
SECOND CANNIBAL CHILD: Neither do I, let's try adding more salt.

What did the vegetarian cannibal eat?
Swedes.

'Waiter, there's a hand in my soup!'
'That's not your soup, sir, that's the finger bowl.'

What did the cannibal eat when he was on a diet?
Pygmies.

A cannibal bold of Penzance
Ate an uncle and two of his aunts,
A cow and her calf,
An ox and a half –
And now he can't button his pants.

What did the cannibal say as he put down the saw?
'I've always wondered what it would be like to have a half-brother.'

CHARLIE CANNIBAL: Am I too late for dinner?
CLARA CANNIBAL: Yes, everybody's eaten.

CUTHBERT CANNIBAL: I've brought a friend home for tea, Mum.
MOTHER CANNIBAL: That's nice, dear. Put him in the freezer and we'll eat him next week.

CHRISSIE CANNIBAL: Should chips be eaten with the fingers?
CLARRIE CANNIBAL: No, fingers should be eaten separately.

How does a cannibal greet a guest?
'Pleased to eat you.'

What did the cannibal do at the wedding?
Toasted the bride and groom.

FIRST CANNIBAL: How do you know our new missionary has been eaten?
SECOND CANNIBAL: Inside information.

What happened to the cannibals who ate a comedian?
They had a feast of fun.

SIGN IN A CANNIBAL'S RESTAURANT: Try our tongue sandwiches. They speak for themselves.

FIRST CANNIBAL: Have you lost your appetite?
SECOND CANNIBAL: No, I'm just fed up with people.

A cannibal came home from a hard day in the jungle and walked into his hut to see a cobra curled up on the kitchen table and a very small man sitting shivering in the corner. His wife was busy rolling out pastry.

'Oh, no,' he groaned, 'not snake and pygmy pie *again*!'

MOTHER CANNIBAL TO CHILD: How many times have I told you not to speak with someone in your mouth!

'Mummy, Mummy, why is Daddy so tough?'
'I don't know, but if he's that bad then just eat the vegetables.'

'Mummy, Mummy, I don't like the look of our new neighbour.'
'Neither do I, dear, let's pour some more gravy over him.'

FIRST CANNIBAL: We had burglars last night.
SECOND CANNIBAL: Nice?
FIRST CANNIBAL: Not bad, but we preferred the missionaries.

What did the cannibal say after he'd eaten the comedian?
'I've got a funny feeling in the pit of my stomach.'

What's a cannibal's favourite wine?
One with plenty of body.

FIRST CANNIBAL: Does your wife cook by gas or electricity?
SECOND CANNIBAL: I don't know, I've never tried to cook her.

Nastier and Nastier

How did the dentist become a brain surgeon?
His drill slipped.

What happened when the fat man was run over
by the steam roller?
It proved he had plenty of guts.

Her death it brought us bitter woe,
Yea, to the heart it wrung us.
And all because she didn't know
A mushroom from a fungus.

What was Dr Jekyll's favourite game?
Hyde and seek.

Why did Henry VIII have so many wives?
He liked to chop and change.

What do surgeons do with their mistakes?
Bury them.

What's the difference between Andrew Lloyd
Webber and a corpse?
One composes, the other decomposes.

TEACHER: Name a deadly poison.
SUSIE: Parachute.
TEACHER: Parachute? That's not a poison.
SUSIE: But one drop and you're dead, Miss.

What's a guillotine?
A pain in the neck.

What's a gallows?
A place where no noose is good noose.

Who hit J.R. with a tomahawk?
Sioux Ellen.

'Mummy, Daddy's going out!'
'Pour some more petrol on him then.'

What do you call a corpse who rings doorbells?
A dead ringer.

What did the executioner write at Christmas?
A chopping list.

NURSE: First the bad news, Mrs Addlepate. I'm afraid your husband has passed on. But the good news is the man in the next bed wants to buy his dressing-gown and slippers.

NOTE FOR COOKS: A very nourishing broth can be made of the remains if there is a sick person in the household.

What did one vulture say to another?
'I've a bone to pick with you.'

'Now, Sarah, be a good girl and tell me where you buried Daddy. He has the car keys in his pocket.'

GRAFFITI: Death is Nature's way of telling you to slow down.

Dr Guillotine invented the best cure for dandruff.

In the family's drinking well
Billy pushed his sister, Nell.
She's there yet, because it killed her.
Now we'll have to use a filter.

HUSBAND, AT BEDSIDE OF SICK WIFE: Is there no hope?
DOCTOR: That depends on what you're hoping for.

MR BIRD: You say your first two wives died from eating poisoned shellfish, and your third fell under a bus. Odd, isn't it?
MR NEED: Not really. She wouldn't eat the shellfish.

BARBER: Were you wearing a red tie when you came in?
CUSTOMER: No.
BARBER: Oh dear, my razor must have slipped.

Billy, with a taste for gore,
Nailed his sister to the door.
Mother said, with humour quaint,
'Billy, dear, don't spoil the paint.'

Algy met a bear,
The bear met Algy.
The bear was bulgy –
The bulge was Algy.

What were Tarzan's last words?
'Who greased that vine?'

ANNA: Why don't you marry Archibald?
HANNAH: He said he'd die if I didn't, so I wanted to wait and see what happened.

SARAH: Why did you come home early from your holidays?
SUSIE: We stayed on a farm. The first day a calf died and we had stewed veal for supper. The second day a sheep died and we had roast lamb. The third day a pig died and we had pork chops. The fourth day the farmer died and we left.

Monster Mirth

How can you tell if there's a monster in your fridge?
You can't shut the door.

Did you hear about the monster who wasn't pretty and wasn't ugly?
He was pretty ugly.

How does the Abominable Snowman get to work?
By icicle.

What country do Abominable Snowmen come from?
Chile.

What's a head banger?
A monster with a sausage on its head.

Did you hear about the monster who sent his photograph to a Lonely Hearts Club?
They wrote back saying they weren't that lonely.

Why did Frankenstein's monster get indigestion?
He bolted his food down.

What does an Abominable Snowman have for lunch?
Ice burgers.

FIRST MONSTER: I was so embarrassed when they asked me to take off my mask at the Hallowe'en party.
SECOND MONSTER: Why?
FIRST MONSTER: I wasn't wearing one.

How does a monster sharpen its appetite?
Eats razor blades.

BILL: I saw a monster with pedestrian eyes.
PHIL: What do you mean?
BILL: They looked both ways before they crossed.

MONSTER: A cup of rat poison, please.
CAFE OWNER: Certainly, sir. To drink here or to take away?

What happened when the Abominable Snowman ate a curry?
He blew his cool.

What goes 'Ha, ha, ha, crash, crash, crash'?
A monster laughing its heads off.

What does it mean when a monster beats its chest?
That it's got heartburn.

Knock, knock.
Who's there?
Fred.
Fred who?
Are you Fred of monsters?

What did the monster have in his glove compartment?
Fingers and thumbs.

Where do you find giant snails?
On the ends of giants' fingers.

Why was Frankenstein never lonely?
He was good at making friends.

What did Frankenstein say when he was struck by lightning?
'Thanks, I needed that.'

Where did the monster have her hair done?
At the ugly parlour.

What does a fiend do on a Saturday?
Goes to see his girlfriend.

FIRST MONSTER: The doctor told me to exercise with a dumbell.
SECOND MONSTER: OK, I'll come to the gym with you.

What do you get if you cross an Abominable Snowman with a vampire?
Frostbite.

What brings a monster's babies?
The Frankenstork.

How does a monster count up to thirteen?
On his fingers.

How does a monster count up to twenty-one?
On his toes.

Why do dragons sleep in the daytime?
So they can fight knights.

Why did the monster give up boxing?
He didn't want to spoil his looks.

Why did the monster go to the psychiatrist?
Because he thought everyone was beginning to love him.

What do you call a kind, good-looking, considerate monster?
A failure.

What's a monster's favourite football team?
Slitherpool.

What kind of planes do dragons fly?
Spitfires.

Has anyone seen an Abominable Snowman?
Not yeti.

What do people sing at an Abominable Snowman's birthday party?
'Freeze a Jolly Good Fellow.'

How do Abominable Snowmen dance?
Snow, snow, quick, quick, snow.

What do you call young Abominable Snowmen?
Chill-dren.

What does an Abominable Snowman do when it freezes?
Grits his teeth.

What happened when the Abominable Snowman had a fight with a monster?
He knocked the monster out cold.

LIL: Did you hear about the monster who was a magician and sawed people in half?
WILL: Was he an only child?
LIL: No, he had lots of half-brothers and sisters.

Where do Abominable Snowmen enjoy themselves?
At snowballs.

Why is a turkey an evil little creature?
Because it's always a-gobblin'.

What did one dragon say to another?
'I keep trying to give up smoking, but I can't.'

MICKEY MONSTER: That girl rolled her eyes at me!
MAUREEN MONSTER: Well, roll them back, I expect she'll need them.

What do you call a stupid monster?
A dummy mummy.

How does Frankenstein's monster sit in front of the telly?
Bolt upright.

Why did the monster get such good marks in his exams?
Because two heads are better than one!

What do you call a monster who has no luck?
The Luck-less Monster.

What do sea monsters eat?
Fish and ships.

How does a monster cure a sore throat?
With a gargoyle.

Why is Baron Frankenstein good fun at parties?
Because he'll have you in stitches.

What's a monster's favourite ballet?
Swamp Lake.

What do you get if you cross a monster with
Father Christmas?
Santa Claws.

What do you buy a monster for Christmas?
Brute aftershave.

What sort of monster lives in your nose?
A bogeyman.

Spell it out

FIRST WITCH: Is it the witching hour yet?
SECOND WITCH: I don't know, my witch-watch has stopped.

ILL WITCH: I'm feeling better now, Doctor.
DOCTOR: Good, you can get up for a spell this afternoon then.

Why do witches ride broomsticks?
Vacuum cleaners don't have long enough flexes.

Why else?
So they can sweep the sky.

If a flying saucer is an aircraft, is a flying broom a witchcraft?

WITCHES' MOTTO: We came, we saw, we conjured.

What do you call a witch who sits on the beach but daren't go into the sea?
A chicken sandwitch.

What's a witch's favourite kind of music?
Hagtime.

What do you call a witch's happy frog?
A hoptimist.

What do witches wear in summer?
Open-toad sandals.

What's a twitch?
A nervous sorceress.

FIRST WITCH: A strange black cat just walked in.
SECOND WITCH: That's all right, black cats are lucky.
FIRST WITCH: This one wasn't, he just ate our supper.

FIRST WIZARD: My girlfriend's a twin.
SECOND WIZARD: Can you tell witch from witch.

What did one witch say to another at breakfast?
'Snap, cackle and pop.'

What do you get from a witch selling washing-machines?
A demon-stration.

74

What does a witch say when she travels along a motorway?
'Broom, broom.'

Why are witches good at markets?
They like haggling.

Why couldn't the witch sing?
She had a frog in her throat.

What are baby witches called?
Hallowe'enies.

Why did the witch fortune-teller give up her job?
She couldn't see any future in it.

Said one witch to another, 'What a terrible winter this is. It reminds me of the winter of 2005.'

What do you give a witch at teatime?
A cup and sorcerer.

What do you say to a witch after you've told her a joke?
'Cut the cackle.'

What do you call a witch who only casts good spells?
A charming lady.

MAN: I'm afraid I've just run over your cat. Can I replace it?
WITCH: Are you any good at helping with spells?

The wonderful wizard of Oz
Retired from business becoz
What with up-to-date science
To most of his clients
He wasn't the wiz that he woz.

What happened when the witch parked her broomstick on a yellow line?
It got toad away.

What do you call a hag who flags down cars?
A witch-hiker.

DINER: Waiter! There's a fly in my soup!
WAITER: That's not a fly, that's the cook. The last customer was a witch-doctor.

What happens when a witch loses her temper?
She flies off the handle.

Why did the young witch fail her exams?
Her spelling was poor.

How do you make a witch itch?
Take away the W.

What's the different between a very short witch and a deer being chased by hounds?
One's a hunted stag, the other a stunted hag.

A man in a remote village was very ill, and the witch doctor was called in. He examined the patient, and said he would go away and make up a special potion.

So he went away, and took six ground-up spiders, the skins of two toads, the tongue of an adder, six ounces of hemlock, half a pint of vinegar, and twenty-two beetles' feet. He mixed all this up and took it to his patient, who drank it down.

The next day, however, the patient was no better, so they called in the witch doctor again. 'Hmm,' said the witch doctor, feeling the man's forehead. 'Try two aspirins every four hours.'

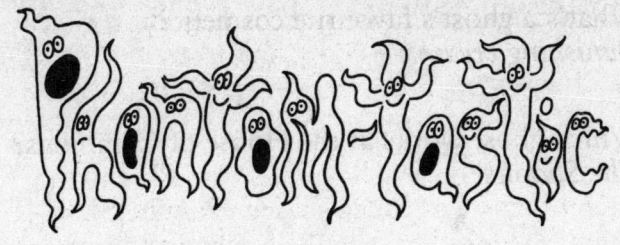

Phantom-tastic

Knock, knock.
Who's there?
Evadne.
Evadne who?
Evadne problems with ghosts?

What does a phantom ride on at a funfair?
A roller ghoster.

79

What's a ghost's favourite cosmetic?
Vanishing cream.

Which ghost works at the House of Commons?
The Spooker.

Which ghost haunts hospitals?
A surgical spirit.

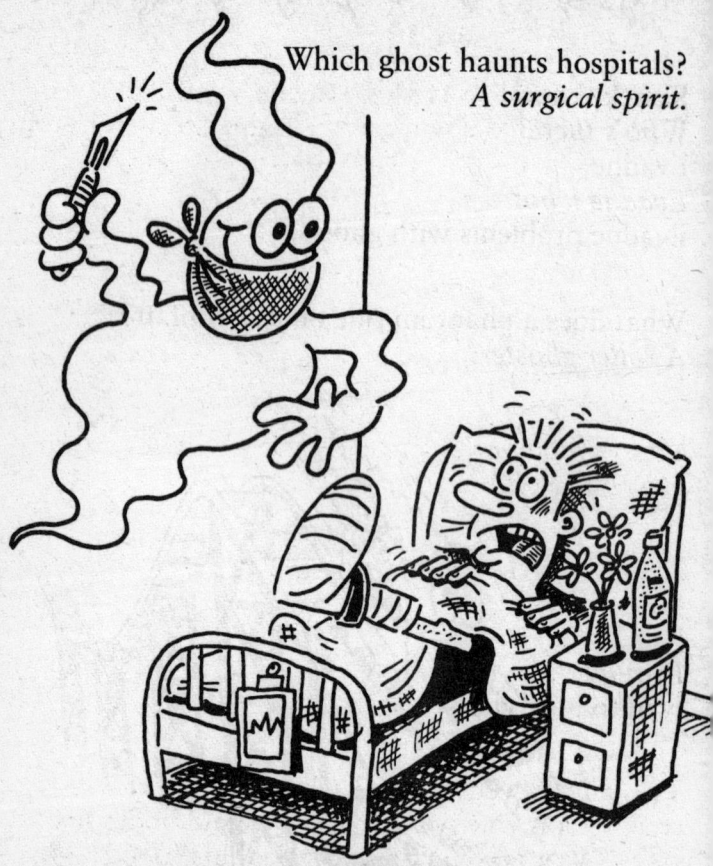

Why did the ghost look in the mirror?
To see if he still wasn't there.

What should you do if you find a blue ghost?
Try to cheer it up.

What should you do if you find a green ghost?
Wait until it ripens.

FIRST GHOST: I'm too thin.
SECOND GHOST: Why do you say that?
FIRST GHOST: You can see right through me.

What are ghosts' favourite trees?
Ceme-trees.

What's a ghost's favourite TV programme?
Horror-nation Street.

What's a favourite game of little ghosts?
Haunt the thimble.

Knock, knock.
Who's there?
Ivan.
Ivan who?
Ivan to hear you scream.

Two ghosts went to the cinema to see a very creepy film. One was so scared he hid under his seat. 'What are you doing?' asked his friend.
   'It's no use,' replied the other ghost, 'I can't watch it. It scares the life into me.'

What do you get if you cross a British Rail
official with a ghost?
A *ticket inspectre.*

What did the ghost of Charles II say to the ghost
of Charles I?
'*You must be off your head.*'

How can you recognise a haunted bicycle?
By the spooks in its wheels.

What do phantom football fans shout?
'*Here we ghost, here we ghost, here we
ghost . . .*'

FIRST GHOST: How old are you?
SECOND GHOST: 547, but I don't look it, do I?
FIRST GHOST: No, but you used to.

Which ghost was President of France?
Charles de Ghoul.

How did Lord and Lady Ghost pass their time?
Haunting, shooting and fishing.

ERIC: I think our school is haunted.
DEREK: Why?
ERIC: Our headmaster's always talking about the school spirit.

What kind of mistakes do ghosts make?
Boo-boos.

What did the boy ghost say to the girl ghost?
'You're so boo-tiful.'

Why was the headless ghost sent to the loony bin?
Because he wasn't all there.

What's a ghost's favourite country?
Wails.

'Did you miss me while I was away?' the Invisible Man asked his girlfriend
  'Were you away?' she replied.

What do you call a ghost who sleeps with the windows open?
A fresh-air fiend.

What do ghosts like to dance to?
Haunting melodies.

What do ghosts get when they retire?
Ghould watches.

What kind of contests do ghosts box in?
Phantom-weight.

What do you get if you take a photograph of a ghost?
A transparency.

When do ghosts play tricks on each other?
April Ghouls' Day.

What do ghost-busters write in at school?
Exorcise books.

What do ghosts do in a car?
Boo-kle their seat belts.

What do ghosts do at Christmas?
Have a wail of a time.

What do you call a ghost shepherdess?
Little Boo Peep.

What did the air ghostess say to her passengers?
'Fasten your sheet belts, please.'

What do you call a phantom navy?
The ghost-guard.

Why couldn't the ghost stand up?
He had no visible means of support.

What does a ghost enjoy reading in a magazine?
His horror-scope.

Knock, knock.
Who's there?
Spider.
Spider who?
Spider ghost in the attic.

When a zombie phones an undertaker, what
does he say?
'Do you deliver?'

What do you call a phantom hen?
A poultry-geist.

Where do ghosts go for their holidays?
The Ghosta Brava.

FIRST GHOST: Your little ghoul's grown!
SECOND GHOST: Yes, she's certainly gruesome.

Knock, knock.
Who's there?
Spectre.
Spectre who?
Spectre of police, you're under arrest.

What happened to the ghost who was a bad actor?
He was booed off stage.

What did the ghost say to its friend?
'I'm sorry, but I just don't believe in people.'

How do ghosts repair their clothes?
With invisible mending.

How do ghosts get through locked doors?
They use skeleton keys.

What should a little zombie call his parents?
Dead and mummy.

What does a ghoul say when he enters a mortuary?
'Anybody there?'

Who appears on the front of ghostly magazines?
The cover ghoul.

Where does a ghoul spend its holidays?
On the South Ghost.

What do you call a ghost who gallops through the desert on a camel?
The Shriek of Araby.

Where do ghosts go at Christmas?
To the phantomime.

What's a ghost's favourite pub?
The Horse and Gloom.

What did the headless horseman say at the department store?
'Take me to the head buyer, please.'

What's the ghost national anthem called?
'Ghoul Britannia.'

On which day do ghouls eat people?
Chewsday.

What shouldn't you ask if you go in a ghost's pub?
'Do you serve spirits?'

Where do ghosts go in North America?
Lake Eerie.

How do ghosts cross the Channel?
By hovercraft.

Where did the ghost of a Red Indian chief live?
In a creepy teepee.

What did the lady ghost wear in bed?
A see-through nightie.

What's a ghost rider's favourite sport?
Fox haunting.

What goes 'Whoooo, whoooo,' and always points north?
A magnetic ghost.

What does a lady ghost put on her face?
Vanishing cream.

How do you flatten a ghost?
With a spirit level.

Knock, knock.
Who's there?
Norma Lee.
Norma Lee who?
Norma Lee I float through the keyhole, but today I'd like you to open the door.

How does a ghost keep its feet dry in wet weather?
It wears ghoulashes.

Why did the ghoul and the demon get on so well together?
Because demons are a ghoul's best friend.

CLIENT: I'd like to contact the spirit of my dead wife.
MEDIUM: It'll cost you £20.
CLIENT: In that case, reverse the charge.

What do you get if you cross a ghost with a sailor?
A sea ghoul.

Why did the headless coachman take a sack of oats to bed with him each night?
To feed his nightmares.

Why was the ghost arrested?
He had no haunting licence.

GHOST TEACHER: Now watch the board, children, and I'll go through it again.

Why was the policeman surprised when a
female ghost was arrested for robbery?
He didn't suspectre.

What do you call a drunken ghost?
A methylated spirit.

DARREN: What's that strange knocking noise?
Is it a ghost?
SHARON: No, it's my knees.

LITTLE JIMMY: Tell me another story about the haunted castle.
MOTHER: I can't, it's a one-storey house.

FIRST GHOST: How did you get that bump on your head?
SECOND GHOST: I was floating through a keyhole when someone put a key in the lock.

What do ghosts like in their coffee?
Evaporated milk.

How did the invisible child upset his mother?
He kept appearing.

Did you hear about the phantom who crossed America from ghost to ghost?

GHOST: Can you tell me the way to Bath?
POLICEMAN: I always use soap and hot water.

What did the ghost say when he woke the man in the haunted bedroom?
'Sorry, I was just passing through.'

Why did the ghost go into hospital?
To have his ghoulstones removed.

What do spooks like on hot days?
Ice-ghoul drinks.

Knock, knock.
Who's there?
Amy.
Amy who?
Amy more jokes about ghosts and I'm off!